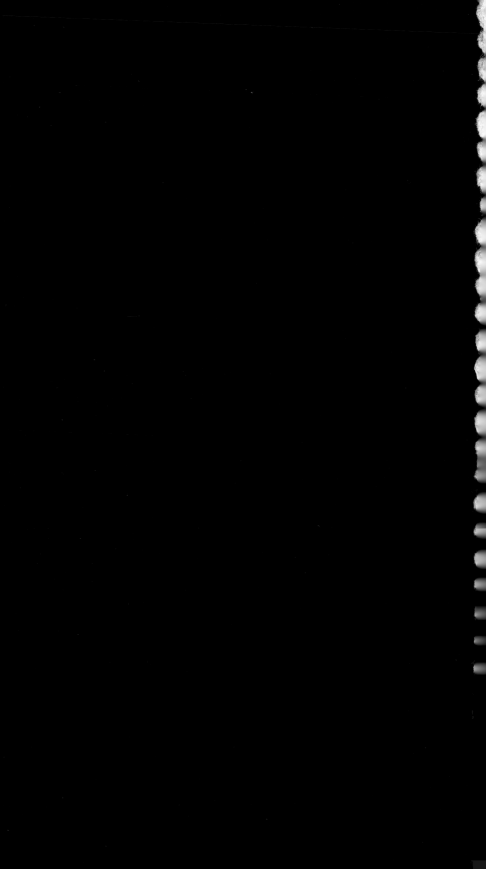

HOPSCOTCH
in the
SKY

HOPSCOTCH
in the
SKY

Lucinda Jacob
and Lauren O'Neill

HOPSCOTCH IN THE SKY

First published in 2017 by
Little Island Books
7 Kenilworth Park
Dublin 6W
Ireland
and
Poetry Ireland
11 Parnell Square East
Dublin 1
Ireland

ISBN: 978-1-910411-93-3

A British Library Cataloguing in Publication record for this book is available from the British Library.

Printed in Poland by L&C Printing

Little Island and Poetry Ireland receive financial assistance from The Arts Council/An Chomhairle Ealaíon and the Arts Council of Northern Ireland.

10 9 8 7 6 5 4 3 2 1

For Owen, Emma and Julia – LJ

For Annette and Ned (aka Mam and Dad) – LO'N

Contents

Preface   1
Introduction   2

Nature Table   4
The Dream of a Plastic Bag   5
I Am   6
Lead Mines   7
Early   7
Cabinteely Park   7
A Showery Spell   8
Bird   9
Rules for a Good Walk   10

Summer Heat   12
In the Library beside the Sea   13
I'll Take You There   14
In the Background   15
Shortest Summer Song   15
99s   16
Outside in Summer   17
Summer Shower   18

Autumn Rondelet   20
September   21
Writer's Block   21
You Can't See Me!   21
Sunrise   22

Classroom Ghost   23

Beware the Ghoul's Lunchbox   24

Hallowe'en   25

Teacher Said   26

Dream Flight   28

Marine Road on a Windy Day   29

That Snowy Night   30

The Shopping Centre

Escalator Blues   31

Rolling Proverbs   32

The Mountains and the Sea   33

There's Always One   34

Winter's Evening   35

Hopscotch in the Sky Poetry Kit   36

Acknowledgements   37

Preface

The title, *Hopscotch in the Sky*, a collection of poems by Lucinda Jacob, tells us straight away that we are taking a journey from the ordinary into the extraordinary; from the everyday world into the world of the imagination. It is an exhilarating trip. Lucinda Jacob lives in the Dublin area and loves to walk about looking and listening. As she says in her excellent introduction, 'Ideas for poems are all around us; all we have to do is keep our eyes and our ears open.' This she does with consummate ease and the poems are an unexpected mixture of the real and the imagined.

There is an unusual range of poetic technique, carried very lightly, in *Hopscotch in the Sky* and a wide variety of subject matter. There are humorous poems, touching poems, some slightly ghoulish poems and other surreal ones – all of them delightfully original.

Lucinda Jacob's writing is beautifully complemented by Lauren O'Neill's whimsical, playful and uplifting illustrations, their rich colour palette reflecting the changing seasons of the poems.

These poems will entertain parents, teachers and young readers alike. *Hopscotch in the Sky* is a marvellous addition to poetry for children here and everywhere.

– Marie Heaney

Introduction

I live in Dún Laoghaire, a large seaside town south of Dublin, and I like to get out and about, to go into the shops and walk in the parks or down the pier. I love swimming in the sea, even in winter. But best of all I like to talk to people and to listen to what they have to say. Lots of the things I do and the things people have said have made me stop and think and some of those things are now in the poems in this book.

One windy day a man really did say to me that Marine Road is the road of flying grannies! How brilliant was that as an idea for a poem? Another time someone said to me that mermaids might come into the new library in Dún Laoghaire, as it is so close to the sea. That got me wondering what it would be like if mermaids really did come into a library. What would it be like if a mythical creature came into a building near your home?

Can you believe that one winter night just after Christmas, a huge deer was seen on our street, in a big town, miles away from the mountains? I just had to write about that!

Ideas for poems are all around us; all we have to do is keep our eyes and ears open. I was walking home one day when I noticed a plastic bag blowing along beside me, just bobbing along and not quite getting off the ground. I thought it looked like it was trying to be a balloon! So I wrote about that. Another time I was walking up on Killiney Hill and for some reason I kept repeating 'under the trees' to the rhythm of my own footsteps. Yes, I'm sure I did sound a bit crazy but that walk gave me the line I needed to start 'Autumn Rondelet'.

Sometimes something will catch your eye – it could be anything, like the raindrop on the leaf in my poem 'Early', and the challenge (yes, writing is challenging and can be hard work) – the challenge is to find the words to describe what you have noticed. I decided to write 'Early' in a poetic form called a haiku, so I had to fit the words into a set pattern which is a bit like doing a jigsaw puzzle but with words.

I like the way you can show how you feel about something in a poem and how you can fit big things into short poems. For example, the huge stretch of grass at Cabinteely Park made me feel like running and I put that feeling into a really little poem. I like the way writing poems gives you the freedom to do things like that.

When I was thinking of making my poems into a book, and I gathered them all together, I noticed how many of them were about the seasons, so I decided to group them like that. This book is a year of poems. See if you can work out where the spring poems meld into summer, where summer gives way to autumn and where autumn falls into winter. Whether you run through this year of poems in one go or dip in and out of the seasons, I hope you enjoy them. Happy reading!

– Lucinda Jacob

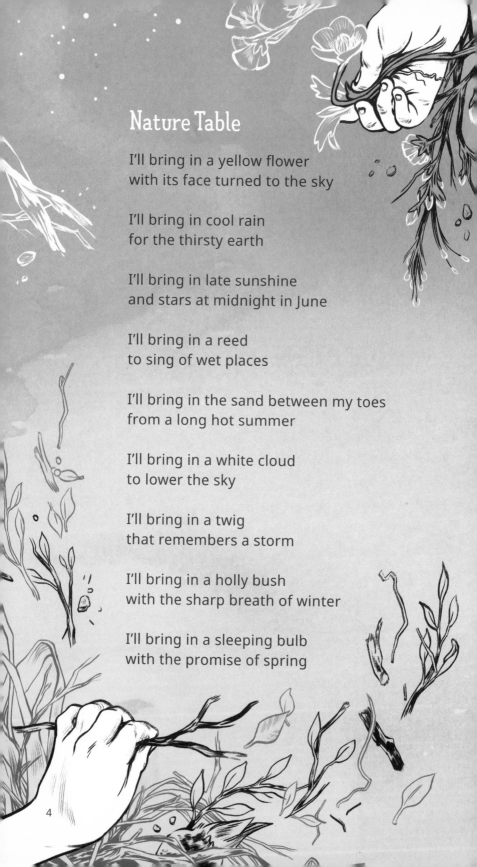

Nature Table

I'll bring in a yellow flower
with its face turned to the sky

I'll bring in cool rain
for the thirsty earth

I'll bring in late sunshine
and stars at midnight in June

I'll bring in a reed
to sing of wet places

I'll bring in the sand between my toes
from a long hot summer

I'll bring in a white cloud
to lower the sky

I'll bring in a twig
that remembers a storm

I'll bring in a holly bush
with the sharp breath of winter

I'll bring in a sleeping bulb
with the promise of spring

The Dream of a Plastic Bag

The plastic bag in the gutter
looked up at the moon
and said, 'Yes,
I'd rather be a balloon.

'Perhaps if I could be
rounder, puffier, stronger,
tighter, airier,
just a lovelier vision of me ...'

A breath, a gust of air
bounced it along the pavement,
lifted it, bobbing and tumbling
lightly along the wall top

and away into the night sky.

I Am

I am a tortoise crawling out of bed in the morning
I am a cat lapping up my milk at breakfast
I am a puppy tumbling in the classroom door
I am an ant pushing my load uphill all day
I am an eagle diving on my snack at break time
I am a lizard snoozing in the sun of story time
I am a cheetah racing in the afternoon park
I am a lion roaring at the top of the hill
I am a bear with my honey at teatime
I am an owl blinking in the twilight
I am a salmon swimming upstream against sleep
I am the dreamer with dreams deep as the ocean

Lead Mines

Up at the Lead Mines
scrambling up the purple hill
we can see the sea

Early

Look how each dewdrop
reflecting on silver grass
holds the whole morning

Cabinteely Park

A grass slope stretches,
runs greenly away downhill
and I run with it

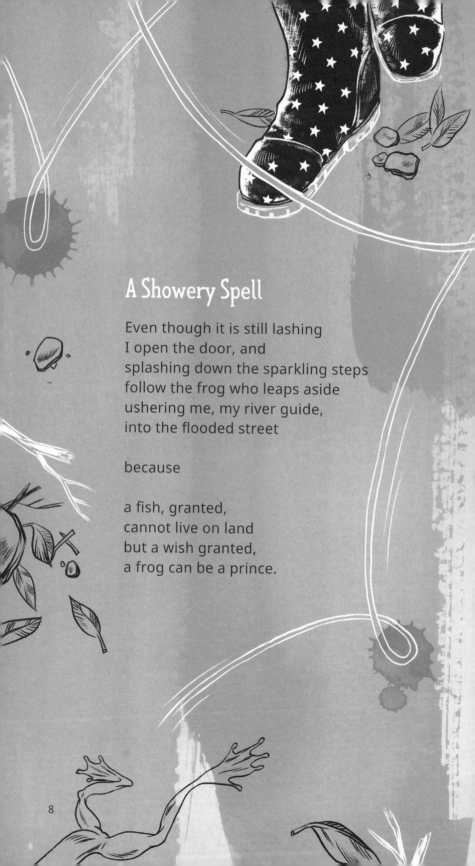

A Showery Spell

Even though it is still lashing
I open the door, and
splashing down the sparkling steps
follow the frog who leaps aside
ushering me, my river guide,
into the flooded street

because

a fish, granted,
cannot live on land
but a wish granted,
a frog can be a prince.

Bird

Sometimes being your best friend
Makes me feel like a little bird
With my beak stretched open
Ruffling my feathers,
Hungry.

Rules for a Good Walk

Come out with me
walk at my pace
talk to me
let me pet the big wet dog
put your phone away
kick up the leaves
and run with me
let me slow down and splash
in the shiny puddle
put your phone away
look at the stone I bring you
show me the beetle under your stone
put your phone away
write my name in the mud with a stick
let me get muddy
let me throw my hat off
put your phone away
put your phone away

Summer Heat

Summer heat for me
will always be
that oozy feeling between our toes
of melting tar
as we,
carrying sandals,
licking ice-creams,
walk barefoot
along the seams
of the baking concrete road.

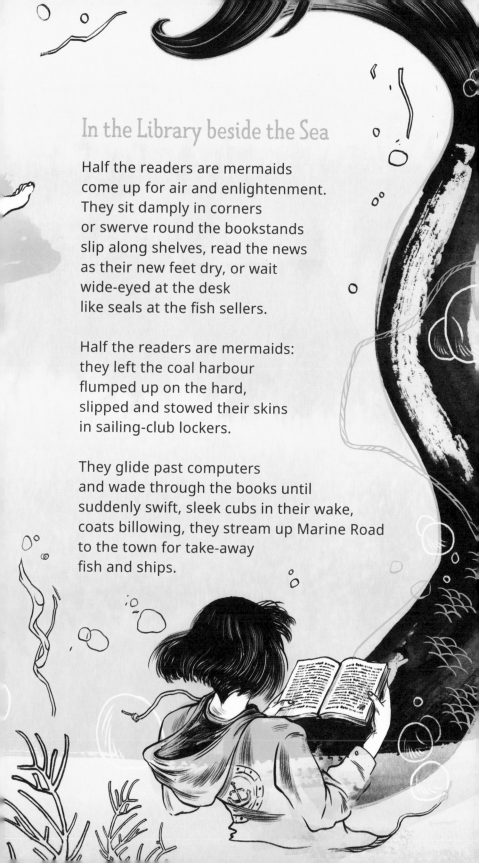

In the Library beside the Sea

Half the readers are mermaids
come up for air and enlightenment.
They sit damply in corners
or swerve round the bookstands
slip along shelves, read the news
as their new feet dry, or wait
wide-eyed at the desk
like seals at the fish sellers.

Half the readers are mermaids:
they left the coal harbour
flumped up on the hard,
slipped and stowed their skins
in sailing-club lockers.

They glide past computers
and wade through the books until
suddenly swift, sleek cubs in their wake,
coats billowing, they stream up Marine Road
to the town for take-away
fish and ships.

I'll Take You There

Listen, the gorse is clicking its fingers
The rushes slip-slipping tell secrets of sedge
Where sheep are maa-maa-ing high echoing air
Grasshoppers fall silent at our shadow's edge.
I'll take you there.

Feel the wet warmth of the bog going barefoot
The flowers that laugh as they tickle our feet
Come with me as the rain starts its dancing
And stroke the damp cloud as it brushes your cheek.
I'll take you there.

Taste the wind with salt in its whiskers
Smell the mint in the air as we step-step the stream
And cut for yourself, breathe a slice of the harvest
The soda-bread day hard-baked by the sun.
I'll take you there.

See the great sweep of the sunset at sea
The shoulders of hills which are never the same
Is it purple of heather or orchid or fuchsia
Or scarlet montbretia or sundew in flame?
I'll take you there.

Let the grass tell you it's you that belong here
The harebells are ringing their lilac for you
The rain it is missing you, quietly sobbing
And the wind it is calling, calling your tune.
I'll take you there.

In the Background

How come there is always a stranger
in every holiday photo?

And how many pics have been taken of me
back to Texas or Kyoto?

Shortest Summer Song

It's cool in a pool.

15

99s

On the seafront in my home town
people come and go like tides,
walk slowly up the promenade,

        and back again.

There's an old man who comes along,
he seems alone but still he queues
for an ice-cream, and then buys two.

        He turns again,

then holds one out for his old dog
and they sit together, side by side
licking the drips, watching the tide

        turn back again.

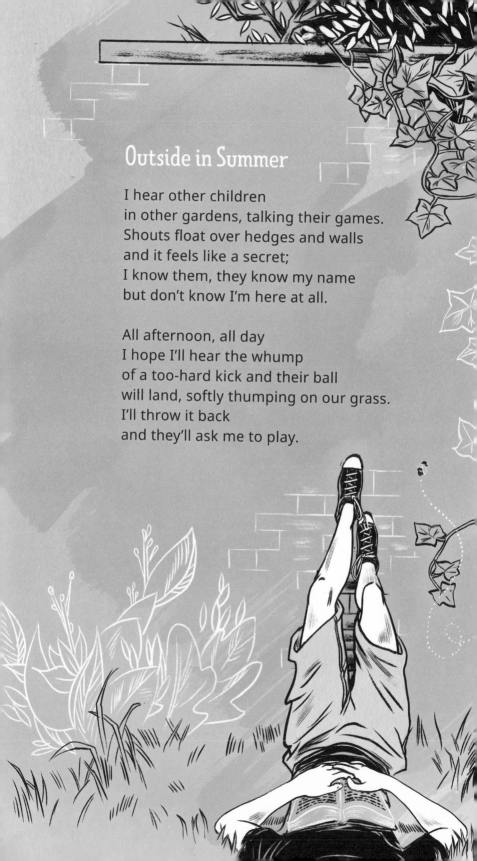

Outside in Summer

I hear other children
in other gardens, talking their games.
Shouts float over hedges and walls
and it feels like a secret;
I know them, they know my name
but don't know I'm here at all.

All afternoon, all day
I hope I'll hear the whump
of a too-hard kick and their ball
will land, softly thumping on our grass.
I'll throw it back
and they'll ask me to play.

Summer Shower

Just a few drops cool on bare arms
and suddenly it's wet: Run! Run!
Pick up the toys that might get ruined!

The rug and cushions –
the teddies, the doll's clothes –
leave the plastic tea set and the ball.

Hurry! Hurry!
Wipe your feet and dry your face,
then from the open door look back out

as the little cups and saucers fill with rain.

Autumn Rondelet

Under the trees
Wind-blown branches litter the ground.
Under the trees
Racing, dancing, the season flees.
Summer gone, mist muffles all sound.
In shafts of light leaves twirl around
Under the trees.

September

Leaves September-gold
soar in the still-blue sky as
we swoop back to school

Writer's Block

2B or not 2B?
That is the pencil.

You Can't See Me!

In school everyone has to be
Good at something.

I'm good at keeping quiet so
No one notices.

Sunrise

Sun rises –
a gold sea path
shines on us through the clouds
then sets the sky over the dark mountain
on fire.

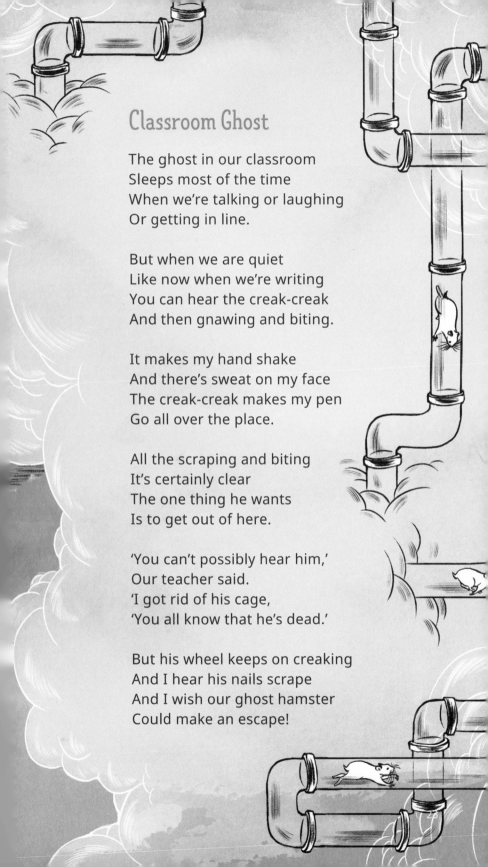

Classroom Ghost

The ghost in our classroom
Sleeps most of the time
When we're talking or laughing
Or getting in line.

But when we are quiet
Like now when we're writing
You can hear the creak-creak
And then gnawing and biting.

It makes my hand shake
And there's sweat on my face
The creak-creak makes my pen
Go all over the place.

All the scraping and biting
It's certainly clear
The one thing he wants
Is to get out of here.

'You can't possibly hear him,'
Our teacher said.
'I got rid of his cage,
'You all know that he's dead.'

But his wheel keeps on creaking
And I hear his nails scrape
And I wish our ghost hamster
Could make an escape!

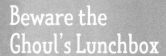

Beware the Ghoul's Lunchbox

Look in a vampire's lunchbox
Lift the lid if you can
on a dripping scream bun
filled with bloodberry jam.

Look in a witch's lunchbox
And try not to sneeze
over snail-shell crackers
flavoured with fleas.

Look in a ghost's lunchbox
You can eat if you're dead
a see-through mist sandwich
made from barely-there bread.

Look in a wizard's lunchbox
If you're crazy you'll find
fizzy-drink fireworks
to alter your mind.

Look in a goblin's lunchbox
This might make you wheeze:
it's slime jelly – sprinkled
with stings of dead bees.

Look in a banshee's lunchbox
You'll shiver with cold
if you taste the mice-cream
with a smear of green mould.

But beware the ghoul's lunchbox!
It's shaped like a tomb.
There's lots of us in here,
there's plenty of room!

Hallowe'en

In the early dark
tiny witches and ghosts screech
joyful at our door

Teacher Said

Bring something in
anything you like –
but not your football!

So in my schoolbag I've got

my football net
some mud and our trampoline

the playground with the zip wire
the shop full of computer games

the escalator in the shopping centre
that speeds up when you step on it

the pier where the seal begs for fish guts
and the pip already growing inside my apple

the tree roots wrapped around a rock
where the rain washed the earth away

the fox trying to reach our birdfeeder
on the stormy night that kept me awake

and my birthday party.

Magic!

Dream Flight

When night begins to fall
I watch the sky until it's velvet dark
and suddenly I know I must step out –
the stars are strong enough to hold me now
and I'm foot-footing it
heel-to-toe, star to star
like hopscotch in the sky.

I pass the moon and find that I – hello! –
am interrupting midnight conversations
from satellites back down to mobile phones.
I overtake a rocket and surprise
sleepy astronauts on their way to Mars.

I wave and entertain them, juggling stars
back and forth, hand to hand
then leave them to rub their eyes
as I run up the Milky Way
into a game of chasing and I'm dancing, tumbling
with dreaming girls and boys across the sky.

As night goes on our dance turns into song
and I turn back and join the birds at dawn
singing in their chorus
as I flap my way
        back down
            to earth.

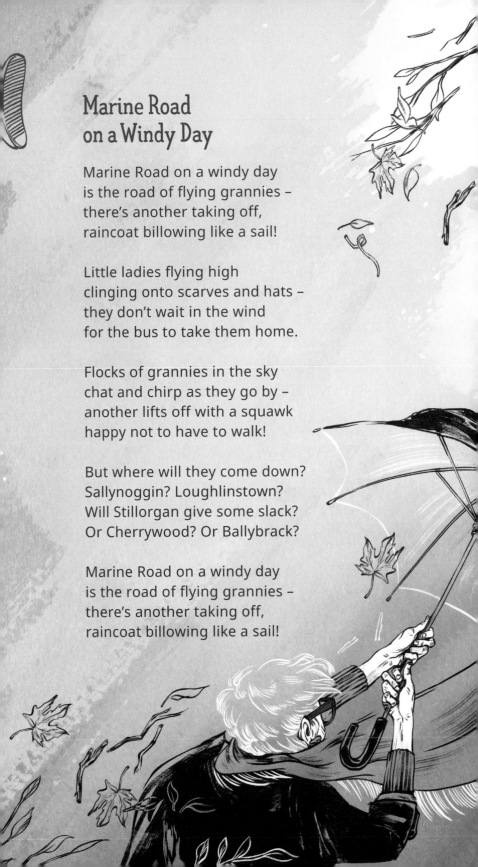

Marine Road on a Windy Day

Marine Road on a windy day
is the road of flying grannies –
there's another taking off,
raincoat billowing like a sail!

Little ladies flying high
clinging onto scarves and hats –
they don't wait in the wind
for the bus to take them home.

Flocks of grannies in the sky
chat and chirp as they go by –
another lifts off with a squawk
happy not to have to walk!

But where will they come down?
Sallynoggin? Loughlinstown?
Will Stillorgan give some slack?
Or Cherrywood? Or Ballybrack?

Marine Road on a windy day
is the road of flying grannies –
there's another taking off,
raincoat billowing like a sail!

That Snowy Night

A white stag stood out
in the middle of our street.

At midnight snow
brought the winter mountains
down to our town.

Trees sleeping in icy back gardens
remembered the forest –
grass remembered sparkling glades –

and a white stag stood out
in the middle of our street.

The Shopping Centre Escalator Blues

My mum, she's buying food
Sis, she's trying on shoes
and me –
I've got the shopping centre escalator blues.

Mum shops as fast as she can, that's true,
but just look at that supermarket queue,
no wonder –
I've got the shopping centre escalator blues.

Now Sis is eyeing up some dudes
and I'll agree, people watching does amuse,
but still –
I've got the shopping centre escalator blues.

I should have made up some excuse:
I've got to leave before I blow a fuse.
I've got the shopping centre escalator blues.
I've got the shopping centre escalator blues.

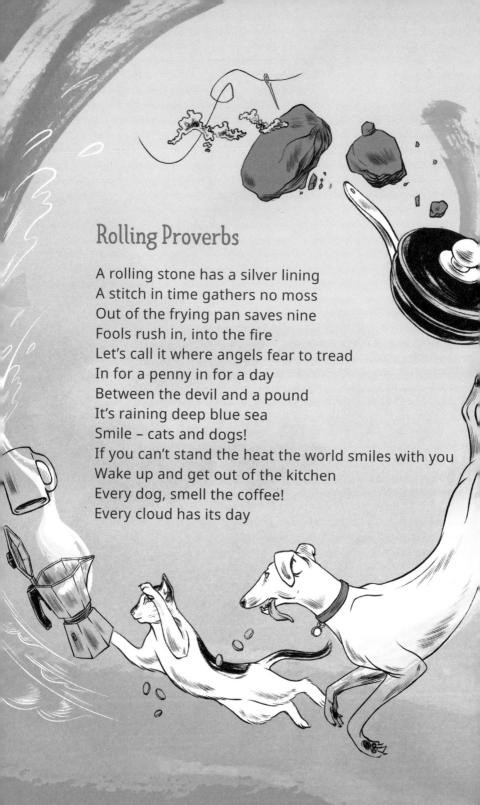

Rolling Proverbs

A rolling stone has a silver lining
A stitch in time gathers no moss
Out of the frying pan saves nine
Fools rush in, into the fire
Let's call it where angels fear to tread
In for a penny in for a day
Between the devil and a pound
It's raining deep blue sea
Smile – cats and dogs!
If you can't stand the heat the world smiles with you
Wake up and get out of the kitchen
Every dog, smell the coffee!
Every cloud has its day

The Mountains and the Sea

We mostly make our homes between
the mountains and the sea.

Some places are too high and cold –
the mountains and the sea –

or raging, stormy, wet and wild:
the mountains and the sea.

Strange creatures are out there beyond
the mountains and the sea.

Huge seals and mermaids, jellyfish swim
the mountains and the sea.

Where deer and goats and wolves might roam
the mountains and the sea

seagulls and swans fly above
the mountains and the sea,

ravens and cormorants call across
the mountains and the sea.

And we mostly make our homes between
the mountains and the sea.

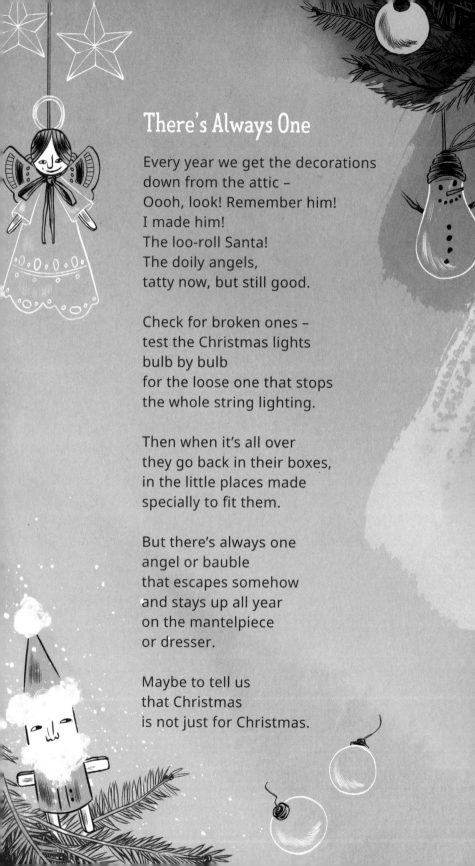

There's Always One

Every year we get the decorations
down from the attic –
Oooh, look! Remember him!
I made him!
The loo-roll Santa!
The doily angels,
tatty now, but still good.

Check for broken ones –
test the Christmas lights
bulb by bulb
for the loose one that stops
the whole string lighting.

Then when it's all over
they go back in their boxes,
in the little places made
specially to fit them.

But there's always one
angel or bauble
that escapes somehow
and stays up all year
on the mantelpiece
or dresser.

Maybe to tell us
that Christmas
is not just for Christmas.

Winter's Evening

Crimson floods the sunset sky
as we say *Goodbye, Goodbye.*

The Hopscotch in the Sky Poetry Kit

Want to write your own poems?

If you're super-smart, you might notice that I have used different forms for different poems in this book – haiku, rondelet, cinquain, for example – and I've used rhyme in some poems and not in others. Writing in different forms helps you to stretch your poetry muscles, and the more you practise different kinds of poems, the better your poems will get.

If you like writing poetry, you might like to learn about the different poetic forms I've used in this book, and get some tips on writing poems yourself. In that case, you can download my free e-book from the Little Island website or the Poetry Ireland website. It's called *The Hopscotch in the Sky Poetry Kit* and it's bursting with ideas for young poets. (And did I mention that it is absolutely free?)

Teachers can use the ideas in the poetry kit in class. Other poets and writers are welcome to use it when they do school visits or are teaching creative writing workshops for children. But mostly I hope that children who like writing poems will enjoy using it and making their own poems.

Download your free poetry kit at
www.littleisland.ie/books/hopscotch-poetry-kit/

Acknowledgements

To Lauren O'Neill, thank you for illustrating this book so beautifully. To Siobhán Parkinson and Gráinne Clear at Little Island, thank you for your enthusiasm and professionalism and for making working on this book with you such fun. To Maureen Kennelly, Anna Bonner, Muireann Sheahan and Jane O'Hanlon at Poetry Ireland, thank you for your work on this book and for the support you have given me over the years through the Writers in Schools Scheme. Thanks also to Marie Heaney for her preface.

To Sarah Webb, a special thank you for believing in my poems and for bringing the idea of this book to Poetry Ireland and Little Island.

To James Butler, John A Connolly, Trisha McKinney, Kymberly Dunne-Fleming, Daragh Bradish, Úna Ní Cheallaigh, Stephanie Joy, Margrit Cruickshank, John Joyce, Roland Evans, Ed Miliano and Marie Naughton, thank you for all our discussions about writing and poetry and for the perceptive feedback you gave me on the poems you read.

To all the children, teachers and librarians in all the schools and libraries I have visited, thank you for your enthusiasm and for the fun we have had together.

To my mum and dad, Thomas and Biddy Wilson, thank you for singing songs and reading poems to me when I was little and for making sure there were poetry books in our house when I was a child.

To my darling husband, Owen Jacob, and my lovely girls, Emma Macnab and Julia Jacob, thank you for all the conversations we've had over these poems, for your insights and for your thoughtful suggestions.

To all of you, thank you,

X Lucinda

Some of the poems in this book have previously been published in the following publications:

The Caterpillar Magazine, issue 4, spring 2014

Taking the Plunge, edited by Vanessa Fox O'Loughlin, Dún Laoghaire-Rathdown, 2014

Read Me at School, chosen by Gaby Morgan, Macmillan, 2009

The Works 5, edited by Paul Cookson, Macmillan, 2006

The Poetry Store, edited by Paul Cookson, Hodder Children's Books, 2005

Poems for My Best Friend, edited by Susie Gibbs, Oxford University Press, 2004

Spooky Schools, edited by Brian Moses, Macmillan, 2004

About the Author

Lucinda Jacob is a children's writer and creative writing teacher. She has written (and in some cases illustrated) several books for children, as well as scripts for children's TV and radio. She is also a textile artist and works part-time as a librarian.

Lucinda often visits schools and libraries, to read and talk to children about stories and poetry, and she often works with children, helping them to write poems of their own.

She lives with her husband in Dún Laoghaire near Dublin. (Anyone who knows the area will spot some familiar place names in this collection.) She has two grown-up daughters.

Lots of Lucinda's poems have been published in magazines and collections, but *Hopscotch in the Sky* is her first book of poems.

About the Illustrator

Lauren O'Neill is a curly-haired, Wexford-born illustrator and NCAD graduate who now lives and works in Dublin. She lives with her husband, Dónal, and spends most of her time in or near her home studio, drawing, eating biscuits or going on nature walks with their dog, Smudge.

She often does drawing workshops for kids, usually learning more from them than they do from her.

She has worked on several books for children, and is the proud winner of the Children's Books Ireland Honour Award for Illustration 2016 for *Gulliver*, a new version of Swift's classic tale.

About the Publishers

Little Island

Based in Dublin, Little Island Books has been publishing books for children and teenagers since 2010. It is Ireland's only English-language publisher that publishes exclusively for young people. Little Island specialises in publishing new Irish writers and illustrators, and also has a commitment to publishing books in translation.

With *Hopscotch in the Sky*, Little Island has realised its long-cherished ambition to publish poetry, and we are delighted to do so in partnership with Poetry Ireland.

Poetry Ireland is Ireland's national organisation that supports and promotes poetry. The organisation has a long-standing commitment to children's literature and to bringing poetry, stories and artistic projects to children, especially through the Writers in Schools scheme, which it has run with passion and dedication for decades.

Poetry Ireland publishes collections and anthologies aimed at bringing poetry to general readers. *Hopscotch in the Sky* is its first venture into publishing for children.